DING DONG MERRILY EATING PIES:

MORE CRAZY POEMS

BY

CAROLYN DAVISON

Copyright © Carolyn Davison 2011

The right of Carolyn Davison to be identified as the author of this work has been asserted by her in accordance with the Copyright, Designs and Patents Act, 1988

All rights reserved. This book is sold subject to the condition that it shall not, by way of trade or otherwise, be lent, re-sold, hired out or otherwise circulated in any form of binding or cover other than that in which it is published. No part of this book may be reproduced, whether by photocopy or by other means nor must any of the content be displayed on a website without prior permission from the author.

ISBN: 978-0-9561573-3-1

Contents

'Twas the night before…
Avon
Facebook
Reminiscing
A woman's work is never done
Definitely **NOT** Politically Correct
batty books

To my parents – without you I wouldn't be here! Love you dearly! ☺

To all my dear friends (old and new), who have seen my 'artistic' potential and listened to my poems – thanks for your support and friendship – you mean a lot to me!

'TWAS THE NIGHT BEFORE…

ODE TO CRISPS
CHRISTMAS PUB GRUB
SANTA'S LITTLE HELPER
SCHOOL

ODE TO CRISPS

Twas the night before weigh-in
And sat on the shelf
Was a packet of crisps
All by itself.
The flavour was cheddar
And onion too
I felt like I wanted them
At quarter past two

I got out of bed
And crept down the stairs
Hoping, just hoping
The pack was still there.
I opened the door
And peeked inside,
There on the shelf
They sat with such pride

The shiny black packet
With writing so bold
Was a brilliant sight
Wondrous to behold.
My hand snuck in silently
To reach for the pack!
I really, just really
Wanted a snack.

With stealth and precision
I opened the bag
And took a deep sniff
Oh what a drag!
I felt really guilty;
My conscience kicked in
Should I decide to throw
Them all in the bin?

Oh what a dilemma
What should I do?
I fancied a snack
At quarter past two!
I think I should trust
My instinct again
And throw them away
And never complain!

So I opened the lid
And threw them right in
To join the biscuits
At the bottom of the bin!
Then upstairs I went
Feeling so smug
I got under the duvet
And felt really snug

Taken from my book – **Larger Than Life on Rollerskates**

CHRISTMAS PUB GRUB

Twas the night before Christmas
And I sat in the pub
Waiting and hoping
I was getting nice grub
I ordered the turkey
And some Brussels sprouts
But there came from the kitchen
One terrible shout

"Everybody run
Nobody stay
The Christmas pudding
I tried to flambé!
I didn't use matches
Nor chef's small blow torch,
I used something bigger
That could blow up a Porsche

"I bought it online
I thought it OK
Until the pudding
I tried to flambé.
It worked on the dessert
The plate and the pan -
The cooker exploded
And so did the fan!"

I looked at the chef;
Hair singed on his head,
His big round face
Was glowing bright red!
With my eyes, I began to
Look a bit lower
Believe it or not
He had a flame thrower.

I've never seen people
Move oh so fast!
Everyone got out
Before the big blast!
All that is left
Of that quaint country pub
Are some Brussels sprouts!
So much for my grub!

Santa's Little Helper

Twas the night before Christmas
and on the mantle piece shelf,
there sat Santa Claus'
Tiny, green elf.
He gibbered and giggled
As daft as could be,
Cos he'd drunk all the sherry
While under the tree!

He rolled round and round
On that mantle piece shelf,
That daft little man
Who was Santa's elf!
He slurred all his words
And swung from the tree,
Played football with the baubles -
Oh dearie me!

He tore decorations,
He ripped them to shreds!
And made ghoulish noises
While the kids lay in bed!
He opened the fridge
And stomped in the food!
Gibbered and giggled
And said words that were rude!

He opened the presents
And spread them around,
But all of a sudden
He heard a bad sound!
Floorboards were creaking
Some one came along!
It wasn't too soon
Before the elf had just gone

There in the middle of
The hulla-balloo
Lay the tired pet dog
At a loss: what to do?
The elf was long gone
To that fairy tale isle,
I can assure you the owner
Couldn't muster a smile

Poor little doggie
Was feeling so blue
Cos the naughty little elf
Had been sniffing some glue!
But there is a lesson
For all who will hear:
Have a very merry Christmas
And a happy new year!

SCHOOL

'Twas the night before school
And lying in bed
Was poor 'little' Johnny
Living in dread!
He sank under his duvet
And tried not to cry.
All he could mutter was
Why me? Oh why?

He tossed and he turned
As he thought about school,
If his peers could see him
They'd say – "You're not cool!
Just stop being a wally
A nerd and a drip
Tomorrow's the day of the
Annual school trip!"

He turned and he tossed
And threw back the sheets!
Sweat on his forehead
And sweat on his feet
He thought of the journey
To Accrington zoo
And wondered, just wondered
What the others would do!

He worried and panicked
And felt for his life.
Until he was prodded by his
Dear wife!
"Now stop being silly,
It won't be a disaster!
You have to remember
You are the Headmaster!"

AVON

ODE TO AVON
ODE TO THE BROCHURE
DING DONG BELLS
AVON WORLD
DID YOU NOT SEE
AVON DELIVERY

These poems have not been endorsed by Avon;
neither has Avon asked me to write them!

ODE TO AVON

Creams in the cupboard
And gels in the shower
Avon cosmetics gives
Each girl some power.
Make up in drawers and
Necklace and rings -
These are a few of my Avon things

PJs in wardrobe,
And soap on the white sink.
Fragrance and powders
Which give out a nice stink.
Splash on for our blokes;
They smell just like kings -
These are a few of my Avon things

Lotions for wrinkles,
And shampoo for all hair!
Of course we look great -
People just stop and stare!
Toys for our kiddies
Lots of shining bling -
These are a few of my Avon things

When the crunch bites
When the bills sting
When things are getting bad;
We take our brochures and put them through doors
Then we are not so sad

Ode to the Brochure

Every 3 weeks
I pop you through
Someone's front door!

You are bright and colourful
And people want some more

You are the window
To my dreams,
My desires,
And inspiration

But sometimes you are just too good
And are full of much temptation

Ding Dong Bells

Dashing through the snow
Delivering Avon books,
Sliding as I go
Over frozen brooks!
Bells on door posts ring
People turn on lights,
I am burning calories
On this frozen night

Ding dong bells
Ding dong bells
Avon calling soon!
The sky is clear
As clear as day
I can see the moon!

OH

Ding dong bells
Ding dong bells
Avon calling here!
Order all your brilliant gifts
VAT's going up next year!

A day or two ago
I took some brochures out
Slipped on the black ice
How I did shout!
People opened doors
And came to have a look,
So I took a great big chance
And gave them all a book

Ding dong bells
Ding dong bells
Avon calling soon!
The sky is clear
As clear as day
I can see the moon!

OH

Ding dong bells
Ding dong bells
Avon calling here!
Order all your brilliant gifts
VAT's going up next year!

AVON WORLD

Some buy from me, some just diss me
I think that's OK.
If I don't give refunds or credit
They will walk away!

They can choose what they can buy
From pages that are bright, that's right!
The customer with the cold hard cash
Is nearly always right! 'Cause they are

Buying from the Avon world
And I am an Avon girl!
You know that they are buying from the Avon world
And I am an Avon girl!

Some like perfume, some like make-up
That's all right with me!
Some don't order from my brochure, I
Have to let them be!

Some use skincare and some use deo,
I just hope they pay!
Only those who spend their pennies
Make my rainy day! 'Cause they are

Buying from the Avon world
And I am an Avon girl!
You know that they are buying from the Avon world
And I am an Avon girl!

Some sign-up and some say no
When I knock at their doors!
Some just can't stop selling Avon
And want to sell lots more!

Reps may come and Reps may go
But that's all right, you see!
Sales Leadership has made me rich;
I'm always on T.V.! Cause you know that I am

Buying into the Avon world
And I am an Avon girl!
You know that we are buying into the Avon world
And I am an Avon girl!

Did you not see?

Did you not see the brochure
I posted it through your front door?
I hope you see the offers
And want to order a lot more!
Oh saw you not my brochure
As it landed on your mat?
Avon sell more than make-up
What do you think of that?

Though not all will look at it
Some may put it in the bin
They don't know what they're missing
The products are so fab!

Did you not see my lipstick
Its bright and shiny wrapper?
And my trendy handbag,
I'm looking very dapper!
Oh saw you not my blusher
Brushed on my rounded cheeks?
I order all the products
Every 3 weeks

Avon Delivery

Ding Dong
There's my door bell,
It's the Avon driver!
Ding Dong
I'm excited now
I'll make more than a fiver!

Chorus
Lipsticks and shower gels,
and things to make you smell nice,
and all at one decent price!

Ding Dong
I am at your door
Holding out your shampoo!
Ding Dong
I give you a book
And say one big huge
THANK YOU!

Chorus

FACEBOOK, X FACTOR AND THINGS INANE

ODE TO FACEBOOK
WHAT SHALL I PUT ON MY FACEBOOK PROFILE?
X FACTOR BLUES
ODE TO WARGAMERS' WIVES AND PARTNERS

ODE TO FACEBOOK

Did you not see my profile?
I changed the picture last week!
I have two thousand and one friends,
And the information I did tweak
O saw you not my profile
On your computer screen?
I am the one with glasses
Who sometimes looks so mean!

Though they are nothing to me!
Though I never play them!
I have some applications
I'll have them 'til I die!

Saw you not my profile?
I'm now a right wing Jedi!
My photos look so crazy,
Because they've all got red eyes!
But saw you not my profile?
Just look at it again,
I'm the one with frown lines
Who looks a bit insane!

WHAT SHALL I PUT ON MY FACEBOOK PROFILE?

What shall I put on my Facebook status?
What shall I put on my Facebook status?
What shall I put on my Facebook status?
In the early hours of morning!

Hurrah and up I post it!
Hurrah and up I post it!
Hurrah and up I post it!
In the early hours of morning!

Shall I put something inane?
Shall I put my life is mundane?
Shall I put I'm feeling insane?
In the early hours of morning!

Hurrah and up I post it!
Hurrah and up I post it!
Hurrah and up I post it!
In the early hours of morning!

I can't stand my Aunty Netta,
If I post it I'll feel better,
But I may get a nasty letter!
Through the post in the morning

Hurrah and up I post it!
Hurrah and up I post it!
Hurrah and up I post it!
In the early hours of morning!

I shall write I hate my job
And my boss who's name is Bob!
I shall say the temp's a slob!
In the early hours of morning!

Hurrah and up I post it
Hurrah and up I post it
Hurrah and up I post it
In the early hours of morning!

Oh dear I've got a text
From the boss – he's not impressed!
I am feeling very stressed,
I have no job in the morning

Hurrah and up I post it!
Hurrah and up I post it!
Hurrah and up I post it!
In the early hours of morning!

X Factor Blues

I'm sitting in the waiting area,
Nerves as strong as steel!
I know that I can win this year
I have the X Factor, for real!

I have my number on my chest;
My spandex suit squeezed on!
And I am ready to go in there,
And sing that blessed song

I know I am simply the best!
My voice as unique as can be!
I know that I will be signed up!
When the judges listen to me!

I get up when my number's called,
I stride right through the door;
I know that when I've finished
They'll be begging me for more!

I go and stand upon the X,
And give them all, my name!
I tell them I am good enough
For glory and for fame!

They ask me who I think I'm like.
I answer, just like Elvis!
I open up my mouth to sing,
And wiggle my enormous pelvis

A sound comes out, I think it's good!
The judges disagree;
Simon Cowell says I am naff
The others don't like me!

I strut up to the desk they're by
To give a piece of my mind!
I curse and swear and ask them
"How can you be unkind?"

"I've 'ad singing lessons since I were 2,
My mum thinks I am great!
So what do all you judges know?"
I really am irate!

Simon says, "Well look you see
Talent you surely lack!
Please choose a different career
And don't ever come back!"

I say "I'll make a million quid
I don't need folks like you,
Telling me how to sing!
There's nothing else I wanna do!"

Then pipes up Louie Walsh and says
"But you're completely duff -
By the time you'd got through half your song
I'd really had enough!"

Cheryl in her gentle tones
Tries to make my spirits lift,
And says, "You cannot sing my dear
But you must have another gift!"

My heart is broken, my dreams in tatters
I really wanted that record deal!
I feel right down in those awful dumps -
No-one knows how I feel.

I go out of the audition place,
Knowing I've made a boob!
But you know what, I got internet fame -
Cos my audition's on Youtube!

ODE TO WARGAMERS' WIVES AND PARTNERS

Where, Oh where has my mascara brush gone?
Where, Oh where can it be?
Oh no my hubby's painted it green -
And it's become a pine tree!

Where, Oh where have my cotton balls gone?
I'm starting to feel depressed!
My kids are using them in a game
To show their tanks are suppressed!

Where, Oh where has my blue sheet gone?
Where, Oh where can it be?
It's covered in small grey battle ships -
It's being used for the sea!

Where, Oh where have my carpet tiles gone?
My head is just swimming round!
I found them laid out on the floor,
Being used as a battle ground!

Where, Oh where are my toothpaste lids?
I left them there, I thought!
Oh no don't say it, they're going to be used
To represent a fort!

Where, oh where have my metal tins gone?
I thought they were really ace!
Oh please don't tell me there's figures inside,
Held down with magna-base!

Where, Oh where has my pan scourer gone?
I'm tipping over the edge!
Hubby's covered it in green flock,
To stand in for a hedge!

DIETING BLUES and HOUSEWORK

Before the summer
Dieters' A-B-C
Exercise A-B-C
Creepy Crawly Critters
Fleas on the Moggies
The Basket

BEFORE THE SUMMER

Before the summer my diet was fine;
I had cut back on biscuits and wine!
I exercised daily, ran everywhere,
Bounced all around like a mad March hare.

Then came the holidays, things just relaxed;
Biscuits and crisps in over-sized packs!
Out went the exercise, portion pots® too!
I thought it was feeding time in the zoo

I sat on my bottom, faffing about,
Not doing much, never going out!
Watching the TV til midnight was past!
Oh no my colours are nailed to the mast

Muffin top growing over waist band,
The elastic skirts begin to expand!
My knickers are starting to leave a nice rim
At the top of my hips! Oh what a sin!

Now I have gained and can't see a way out,
I want to scream and I want to shout!
I need to get focused and plan every day
To see those inches melt far away!

Dieters' A-B-C

A is for Aerobics we know we must do
B is for Bacon - one rasher or two?
C is for Confidence which we see grow
D is for Diet, - that we all know
E is for Eager when we lose those pounds
F is for Fun things - like spinning around
G is for Grain - whole it must be
H is for H^2O - we must drink plen-ty
I is for Interesting - some recipes are
J is for Jumping just like a star
K is for Kit we must take to the gym
L is for Leaner - we want to be thin
M is for Measure, we do this each week
N is for Nutrition bars - which are really sweet
O is for Organic - to help us along
P is for Porridge - you just can't go wrong
Q is for Quality – like low fat steak
R is for Rules – which we mustn't break
S is for Sandwich - please skip the spreads
T is for Tandoori with low fat naan breads
U is for Unique - just like low fat puds
V is for Virtuous - when we are good
W is for Walking - it strengthens the heart
X is for Xtra good - we won't have that tart
Y is for Yogurt - any flavour will do
Z is for Zucchini - to put in a stew

EXERCISE A-B-C

A for Aerobics it gets the heart pumping
B for Bungy come on let's get jumping
C for Cardio - we must keep it strong
D for Drumming and singing a song
E for Exercise it keeps us quite trim
F for Foxtrot let's dance til we're slim
G for Golf let's stay under par
H for Hockey don't hit it too far
I for Interesting - exercise must be
J for Jumping but not out of a tree
K for Kite-flying high up in the sky
L for Lunging - it's good for the thighs
M for Marathon - don't forget to train
N for Netball, but not in the rain
O for Octopushy in your local pool
P for Polo - riding horses, how cool
Q for Queen of the disco you are
R for Rumba - Oh what a star
S for Salsacise - with a Latino theme
T for Tango - with a hunk, what a dream
U for Undoing those couch potato habits
V for Volleyball - jump up like some rabbits
W for Watersports - skiing and diving
X for Xtreme sports - how are you surviving?
Y for Yachting - sailing over the waves
Z for Zumba - the latest exercise craze

Creepy Crawly Critters

I really cannot be accused of hating little creatures -
My house is full of tiny things; one of its main features!

There are dust mites on the shelves,
And weevils in the flour,
And then there are the little creatures
That appear after hours.

There are mice in the cellar,
And rats in the loo,
Cockroaches running around at night
Creating a hullaballoo.

There are fleas on the pet cat,
Worms in the dogs,
Dead pigeons in the water tank,
And buckets full of frogs.

There are bed bugs which share our bed,
Carpet beetles in the rugs,
And every kind of hairy spider,
Living in our mugs.

There are cobwebs in the corner,
Flies on all the food,
Maggots on the rotting meat,
And moths with their brood.

You can tell my house is like a zoo. I love animals you see.
Perhaps you'd like to view them, when you visit me…

PLEASE NOTE THIS IS A PURELY FICTICIOUS POEM AND I DON'T HAVE ALL THOSE THINGS IN MY HOUSE – WELL NOT TO MY KNOWLEDGE ANYWAY…

Fleas on the Moggies

Fleas on the moggies and spiders in the bath,
Come on now nature you're just having a laugh,
Wasps in the honey and bugs in the sink,
Sometimes things natural really do stink!

Mice in the cupboards and rats above ceiling,
My skin is crawling, that's just how I'm feeling,
Weevils in flour and lice in my hair,
Life can be so gross, it just isn't fair.

Moths on the curtains and slugs in the garden,
Where is the mouse trap? Oh do beg my pardon
Roaches on kitchen floor, dead birds in tank
The water is green now and smelling so rank!

When the fleas bite, when the wasps sting
And everything is bad!
I simply keep scratching and scraping myself
And now I am feeling mad!

The Basket

It sat there in the basket
I was scared as can be
Was it my imagination?
Or was it watching me?

I stood there for a moment
Wondering what to do.
What was that in the basket?
Should I call the zoo?

I grabbed the phone and dialled;
I called my lovely mum,
I really needed to find out
From where the thing had come.

"Hello my dear. What do you want?"
She whispered in sweet tones.
"Oh mum!" I cried "Please come here
"To my cosy home!"

She grabbed her coat so quickly
And rushed out of her door
And came over to my place,
So she could find out more!

I grabbed her arm so tightly
With fear upon my face!
I dragged her to the kitchen
And pointed to that place!

"Mum what is it?" I cried to her
Tears rolling down my cheek!
But mum was curled up laughing
And feeling very weak!

After a while she became composed
And gave a great big smile!
"Don't worry my daughter," she said to me,
"It's just the ironing pile!"

Politically Correct?
DEFINITELY NOT!

Where will it be?
Feminine Oppression?
British Justice
Plastic Surgery

Where Will It Be?

Chorus

In the China Sea
With Pakistanis,
Where will the next conflict be?
We've done Iraq,
Now Afghanistan.
Just because of the
Sin of man,
Will China now
Attack Taiwan?
Where will the conflict be?

Where will it be?

Our leaders sit alone
At night and on their throne;
Wondering who they can attack today!
"Oh, will it be a town?
Something bigger to blow down,
We will send the poor soldiers on their way!"

Chorus

Now I wake up every night
Wondering who to fight;
The Taliban or Al Qaeda guys!
Do we shoot them from behind?
I wonder if they'd mind?
Oh boy, they're in for a huge surprise!

Chorus

While I'm always on the line,
Thinking things are fine!
They have shot Osama in the head!
Everyone in the West
Thinks that this is best,
But some Muslims now want us dead

Chorus

Feminine Oppression?

If I wore a burka
You wouldn't see my toes!
If I wore a niqaj
You wouldn't see my nose!

If I wore a hijab
You wouldn't see my hair!
If I wore dark glasses
You really wouldn't care!

I could be invisible;
Be a peeking tom!
Or if I was adventurous
Wear an atom bomb!

Burka, Niqaj, Hijab clothes
Signs of feminine oppression!
Symbols of women slaves, in chains;
Of husband's sad possession!

Is the West really any better? Read on...

If I wore a mini skirt
You'd see more than my toes!
If I wore a jewelled stud
It could be through my nose!

If I did a Britney
I'd shave off all my hair!
If I wore contacts
Would you really care?

I could stand out in the crowd
Be a drama queen!
Get drunk on a Saturday night
You know what I mean?

Mini skirts and skimpy tops
Lots of material possessions;
Greed and lust and gluttony,
Different oppressions!

BRITISH JUSTICE?

If I robbed a jewellery store
I'd get 20 years to life!
But I'd get rather less
If I murdered someone's wife!

If I defrauded lots of cash
The police would be after me!
There are those who get away with it
They are called MPs!

What is British Justice?
Is it just at all?
Especially when the 'common man'
Is the one to take the fall!

It seems, if you're an MP
You get away with breaking laws;
You may even be promoted
And start earning millions more!

Where is British Justice
When a man's shot down dead
By those employed to protect us?
Shooting bullets in his head!

Where is British Justice
When groups shout "Kill the Queen!"?
They never get arrested
You know who I mean!

What is British justice?
I really can not think,
It seems to favour criminals
And those who like pink

What is British justice?
Seems like life ain't worth a jot
'Cept if you steal money or jewels
Your body's left to rot!

So much for British justice
Seems like it's really bent!
And most of Britain's criminals
Are in the Houses of Parlia-ment

Plastic Surgery, For Real?

I'm for real, you'd never guess
What's happened to my chest;
I've had a wonderful boob job
It's the very best!

I'm for real, you'd never guess
What's happened to my nose;
I've had it shaped and straightened!
Just anything goes!

I'm for real, you'd never guess;
I have implants in my cheeks -
I've been saving up to have them
For many, many weeks

I'm for real, you'd never guess;
My lashes are stuck on -
They make my eyes look rather large
It's really not a con!

I'm for real, you'd never guess;
My eyes are usually brown -
I wanted to change their colour now
To match my brand new gown!

I'm for real, you'd never guess;
This hair is not my own -
I've had loads of extensions
To match my skin tone!

I'm for real, you'd never guess;
I went to a salon for my tan -
I look a little orange
That wasn't my original plan!

I'm for real, you'd never guess;
My face has been lifted high -
To take away the frown lines!
The days are passing by!

I'm for real, you'd never guess;
I've got collagen in my lips -
And I've had liposuction
On my overbearing hips!

I'm for real, you'd never guess;
I've got botox in my 'crown' -
Oh dear, when I'm angry
I cannot even frown!

I'm for real, you'd never guess;
My nails are acrylic -
The patterns on them are so neat,
I think that it's Cyrillic

I'm for real, Well, I think I am;
I hope I don't break!
Most of me is plastic
And very, very fake!

Batty Books

Hungry Dogs
By
Nora Bone

Bouncing Bullets
By
Rick O'Shea

Sitting on a Frozen Lake
By
I.C. Butt

Chinese Spymaster
By
Aye See Yoo

Owning Trains
By
Ivan Engine

Digging Gardens
By
Ivor Shovel

Shorts Skirts
By
Seymour Legg

Campanology
By
Isabelle Ringing

Ancient Headgear
By
Vi King-Helmet

Eccentric People
By
Izzie Weird

Cutting Grass
By
Mo D. Lawn

Theatre Seating
By
Rose O'Chairs

Seeking People
By
R. U. There

Prism Perspective
By
Ray O'Light

Perfect Pasta
By
Al Dente

Cooking Pasta with Cheese Sauce
By
Mac Aroni

Glorious England
By
Al Bion

Pseudonyms
By
A. Lias

Running Away to Get Married

By

E. Lope

Quiet Music

By

P. Anno

Watery Milk

By

Di Lute

Going off on Tangents

By

Di Gress

Keeping Things Quiet

By

C. Cret

Perfect Macaroons

By

Al Mond

Sailors Uniforms
By
Belle Bottoms

Stopping Ships
By
Anne Corr

Electronics for Dummies
By
Sir Kitt

Algebra for Beginners
By
E. Quation

The Middle of the World
By
E. Quator

Clergy's Phone Numbers
By
Di Rectory

Making Explosives
By
Dina Mite

Lights for your Bike
By
Dina Mo

Eating Out of Doors
By
Al Fresco

Unaccompanied Singing
By
A. Cappella

Phones on the Move
By
Mo Bile

Rolling Your own Cigarettes
By
Nick O'Tene

Carrying on in Adversity
By
Percy Vere

Sat Nav for Beginners
By
U. R. Here

Combating School Bullies
By
Vick Tim Ised

Catching Thieves
By
Adam Then

Saying No in Russia
By
Yuri Fuse

Safe Moles
By
Ben Ine

How to Take Steroids
By
Anna Bolic

Looking at Roman Houses
By
A. Trium

Controlling Acne
By
Dianne Nett

Tracking Natural Catastrophes
By
Major Disasters

Becoming a Businessman in Russia
By
Ivan Office

Be a Collector of Old Items
By
Anne Teak

Furniture Removals in Moscow
By
Yuri Move

Signs of Concussion
By
I. C. Stars

Gym Wear
By
Leo Tard

Litigation in China
By
Mee Soo Yoo

Walking Through Autumn Leaves
By
Russell Ing

Sinking Ships
By
Lee Kee Boat

Instant Dinners
By
Mike Ro Wave

Playing Music Quickly
By
Al Egro

Stop Unnecessary Food Spillage
By
Celia Bag

Selling Cosmetics
By
A. Von-Rep

Listening to the Dawn Chorus
By
Earl E. Riser

Becoming a Lab Assistant
By
E. Gore

A bit more about the author:

Carolyn was born in Cardiff and grew up in the 70s and 80s in a place called Splott – yep it's a real place. From an early age she started writing poetry for fun, she also writes children's stories – the wackier, the better.

She is married with 2 sons who are taller than her – maybe she hasn't eaten enough pies, or too many! She is a Christian and has home educated since the year 2000. She also owns 2 cats.

She has also published two other poetry books.

She is reading some of her poems on Youtube. To view her videos please visit:

http://www.youtube.com/user/rhyfelwrDuw

www.ingramcontent.com/pod-product-compliance
Ingram Content Group UK Ltd.
Pitfield, Milton Keynes, MK11 3LW, UK
UKHW042318200426
11947UKWH00048B/429